Vol 8

MAZE

FOR KIDS

Ages 4-6

MAZE BOOK

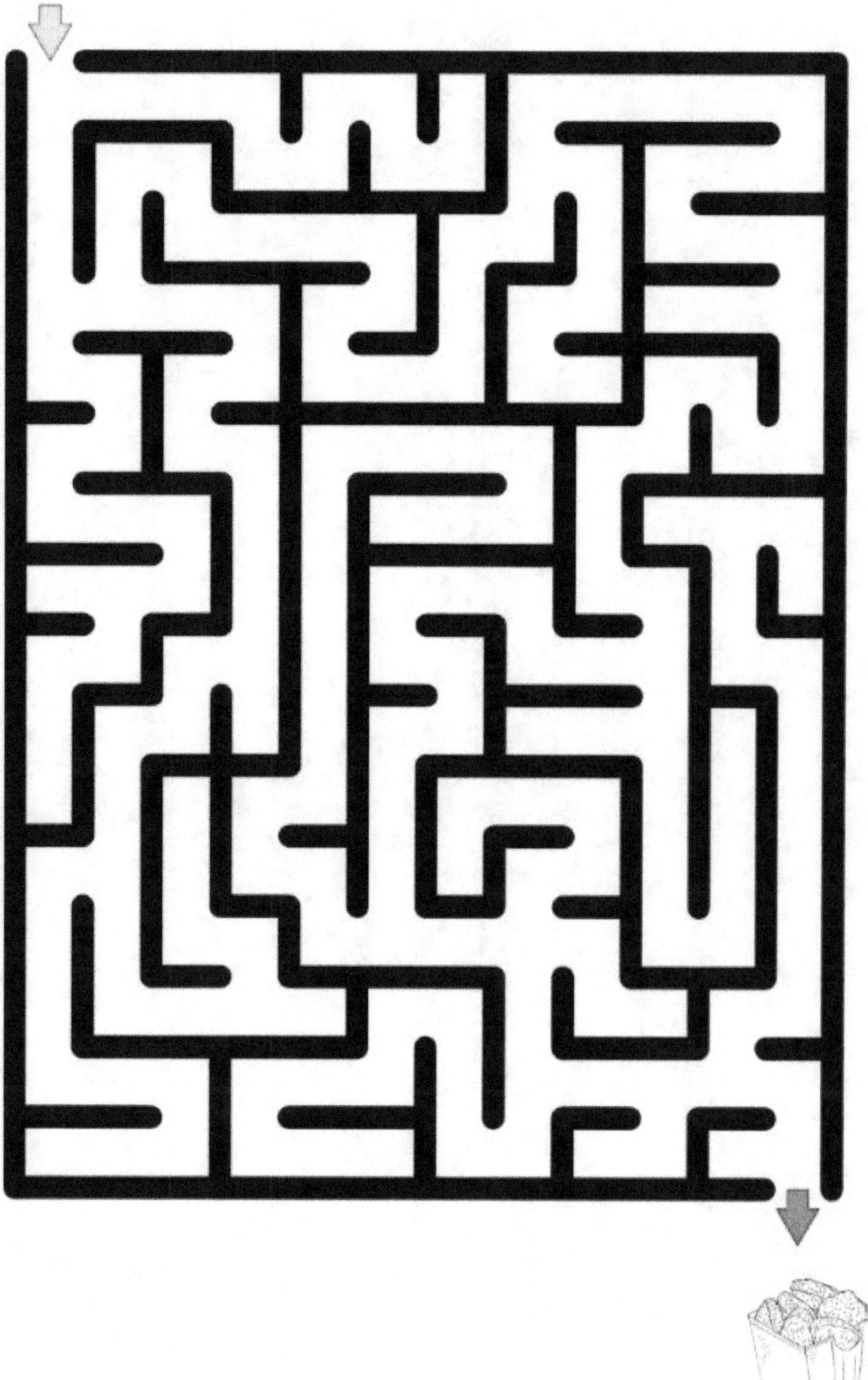

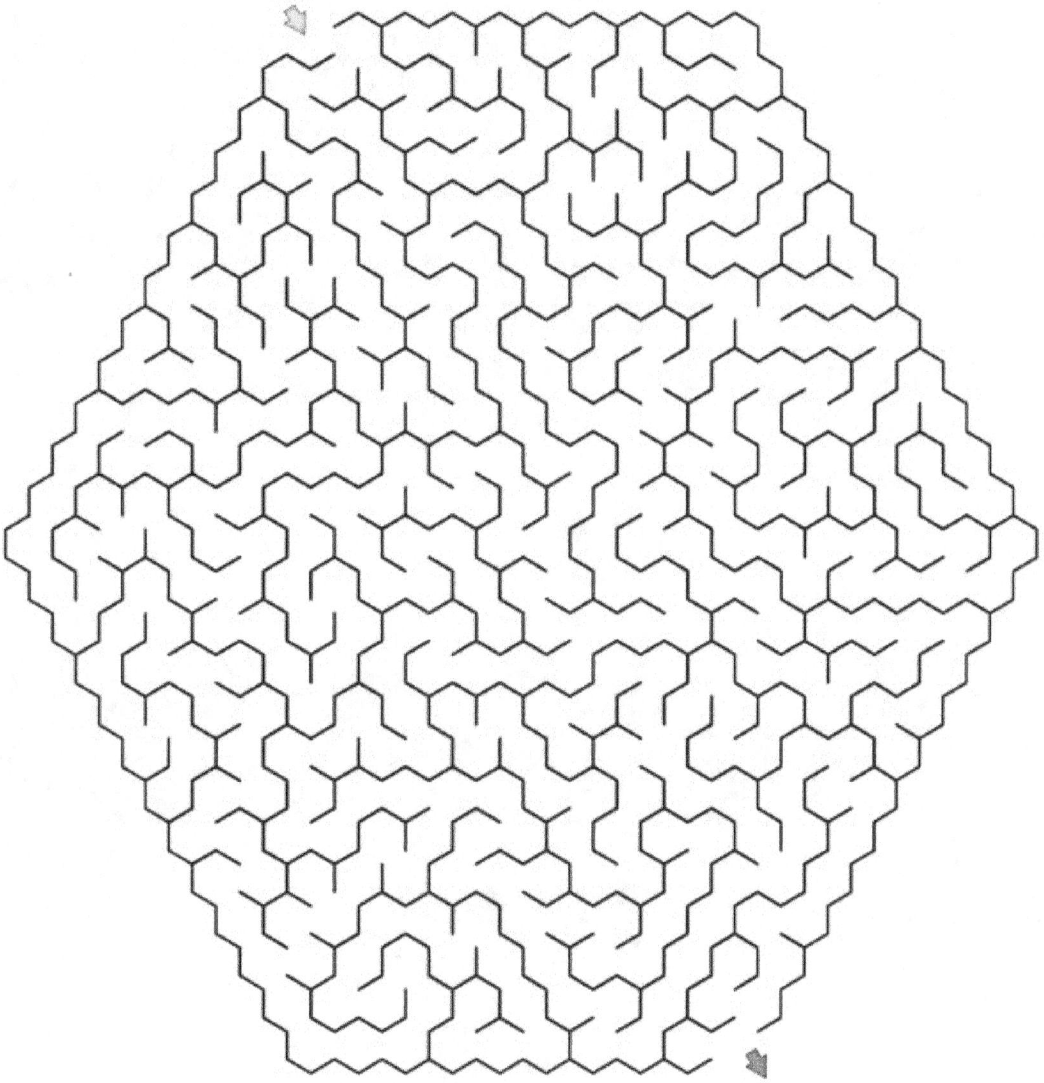

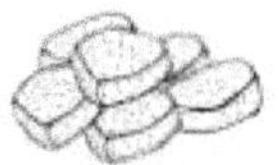

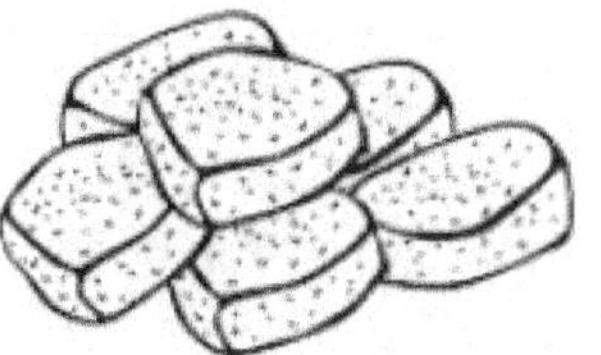

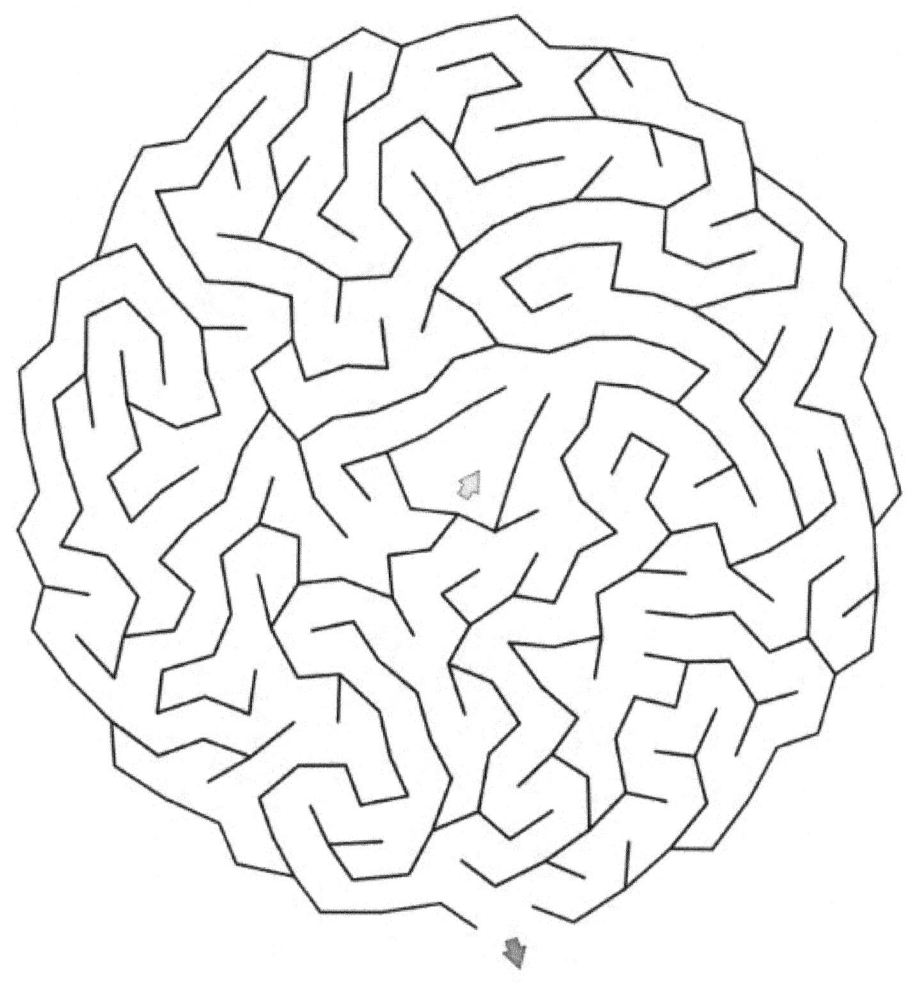

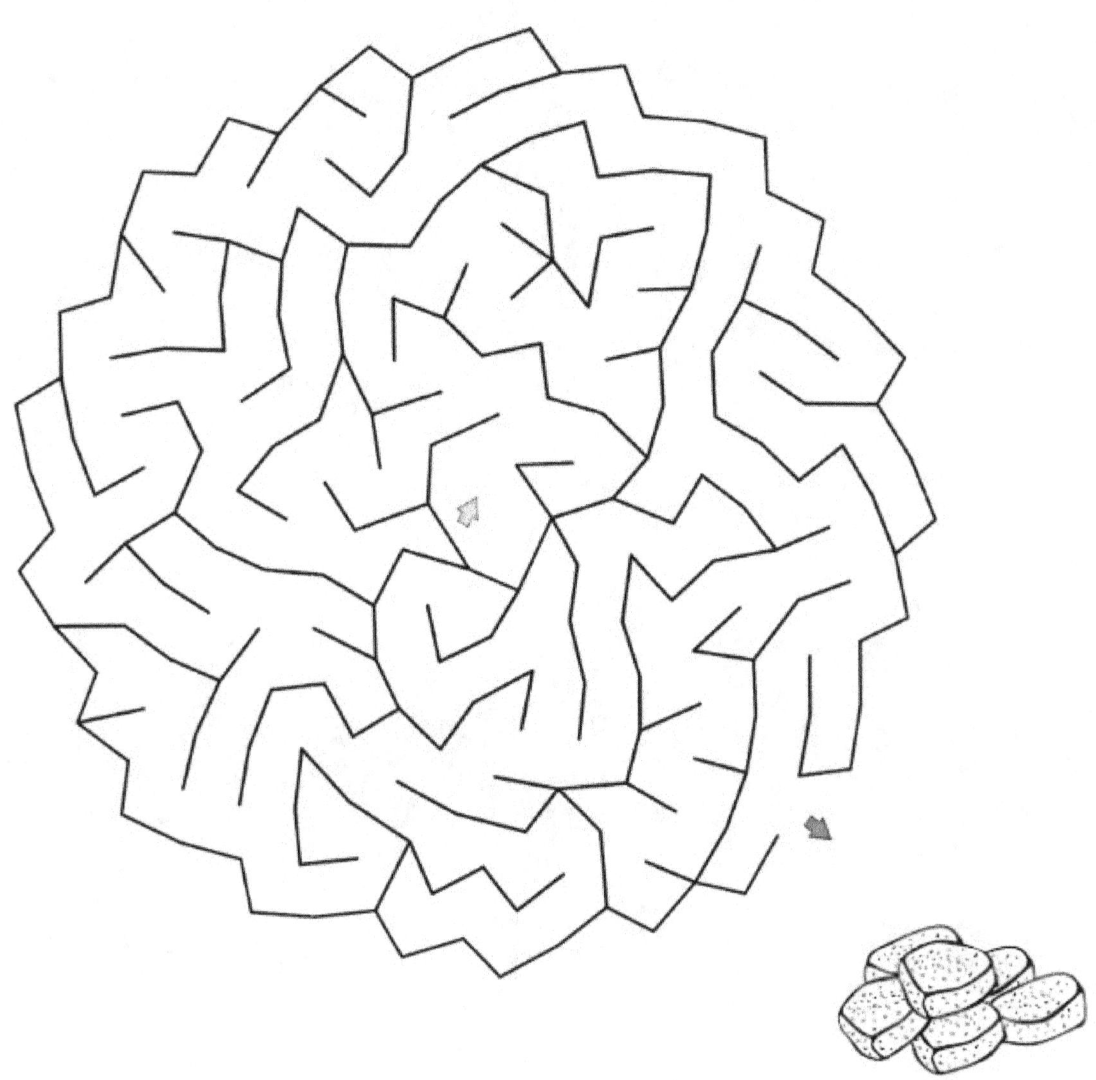

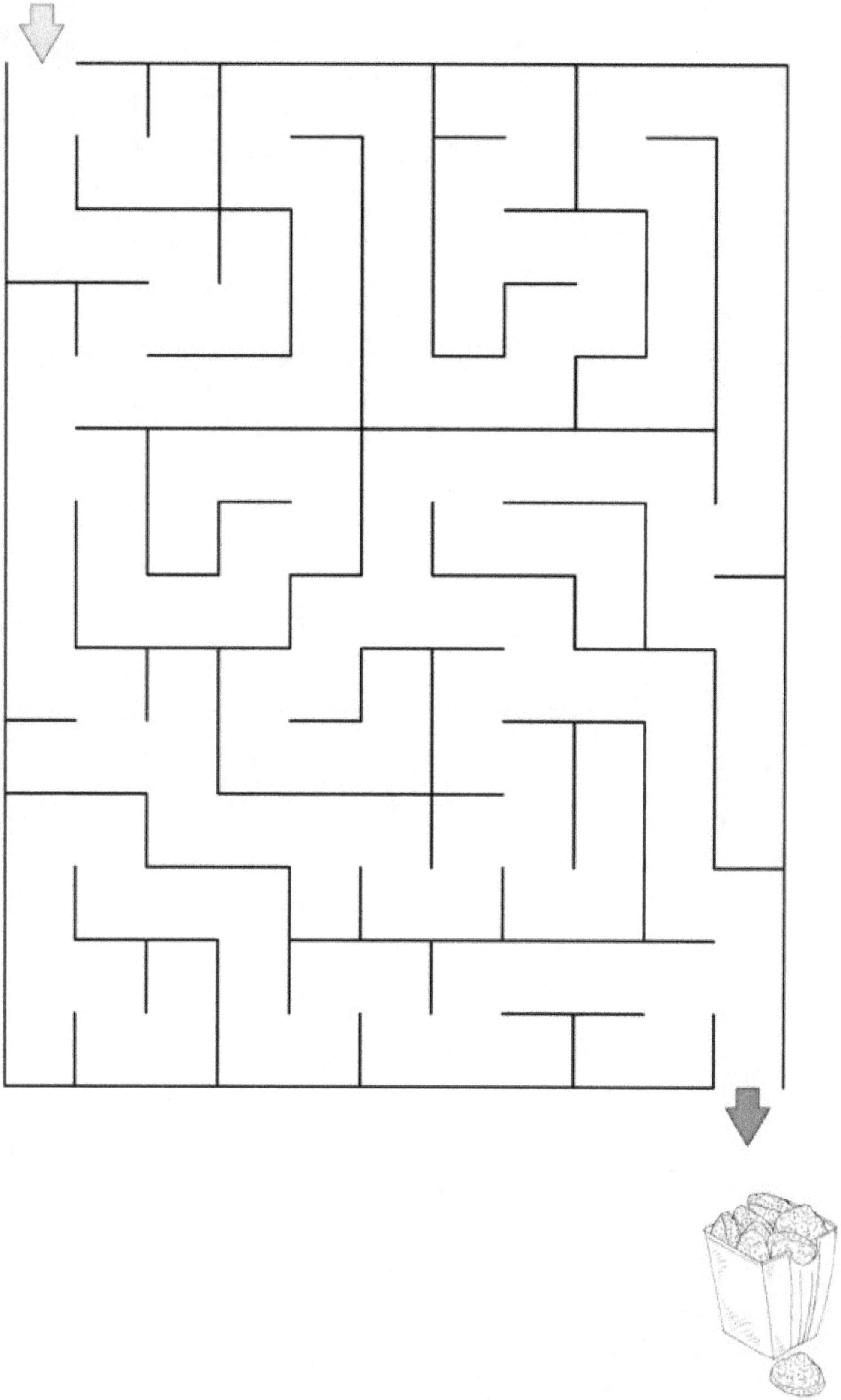

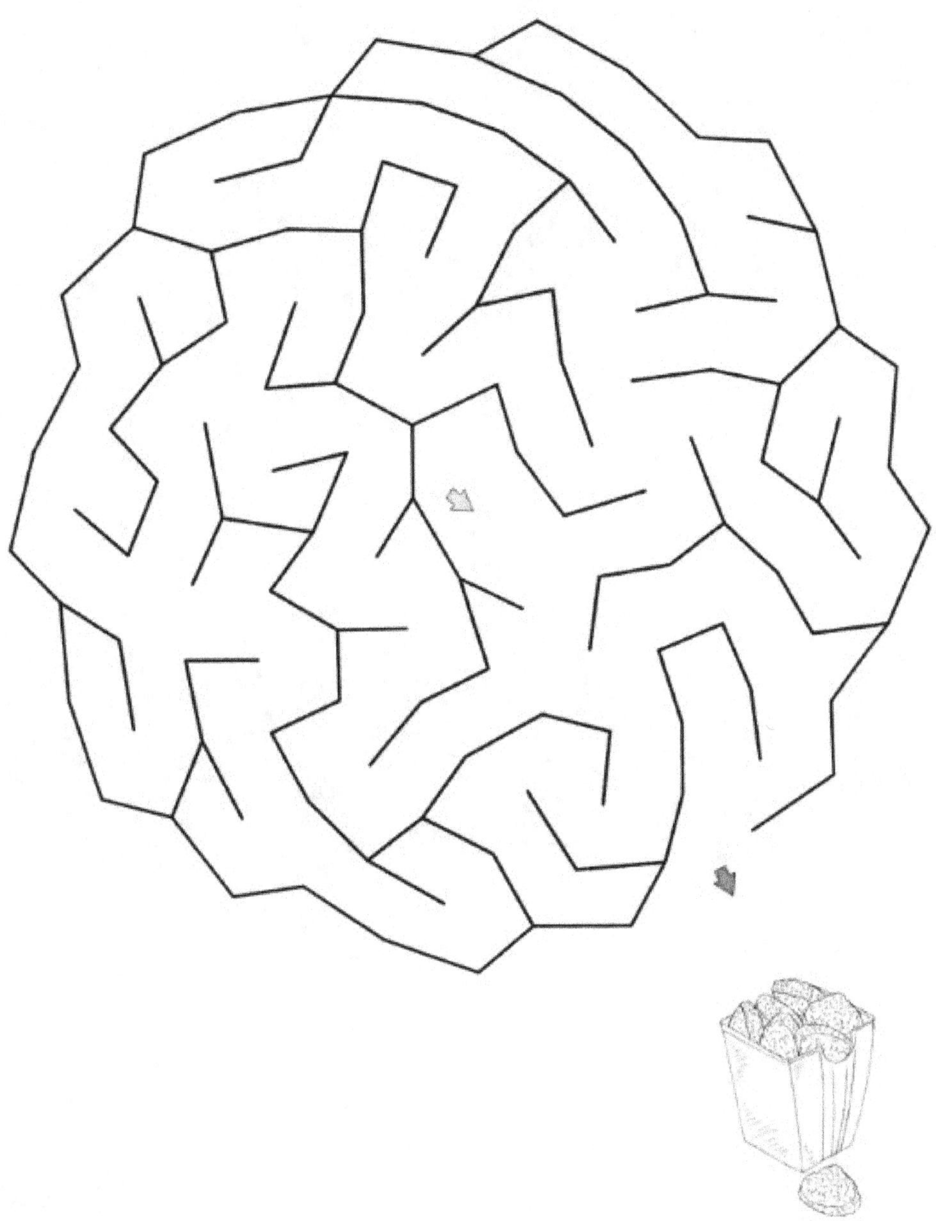

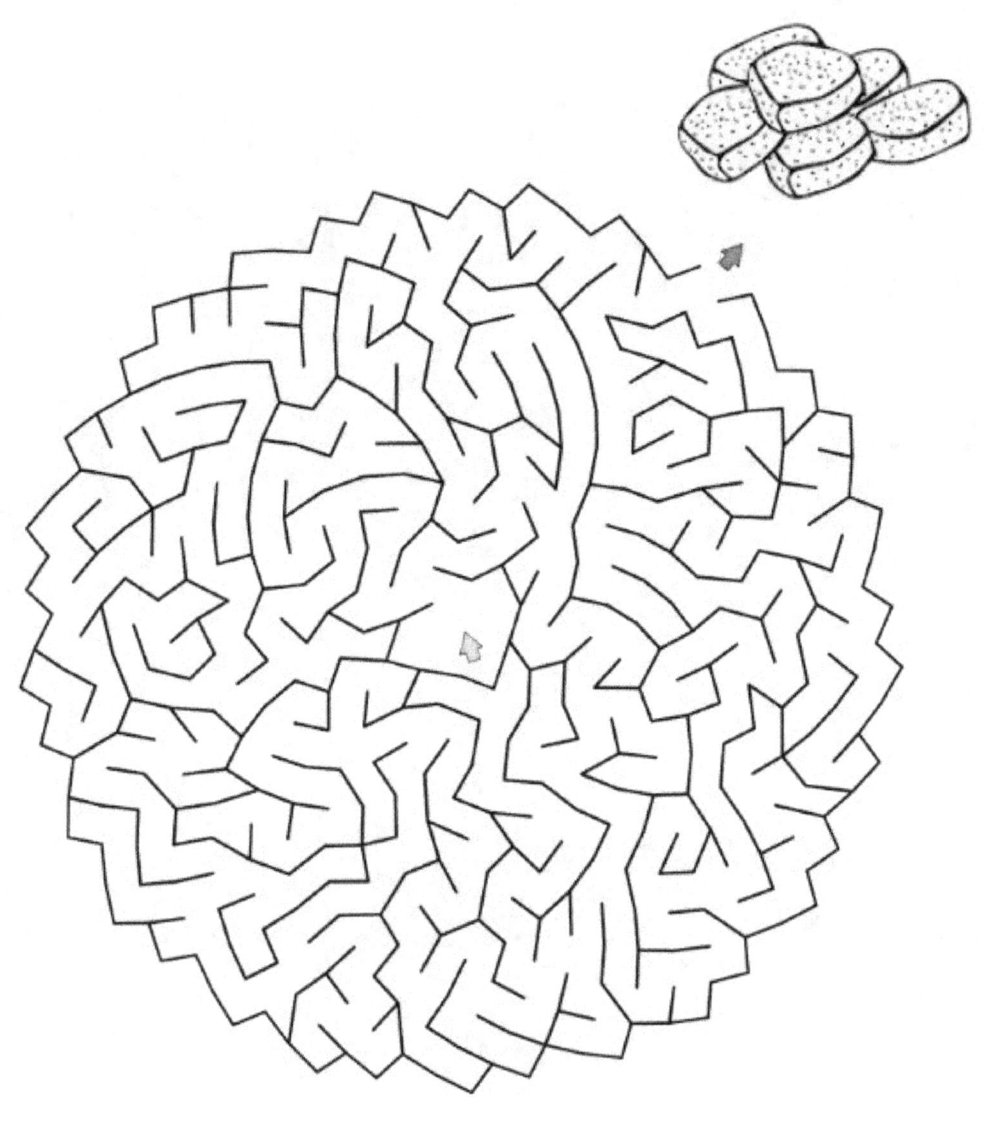

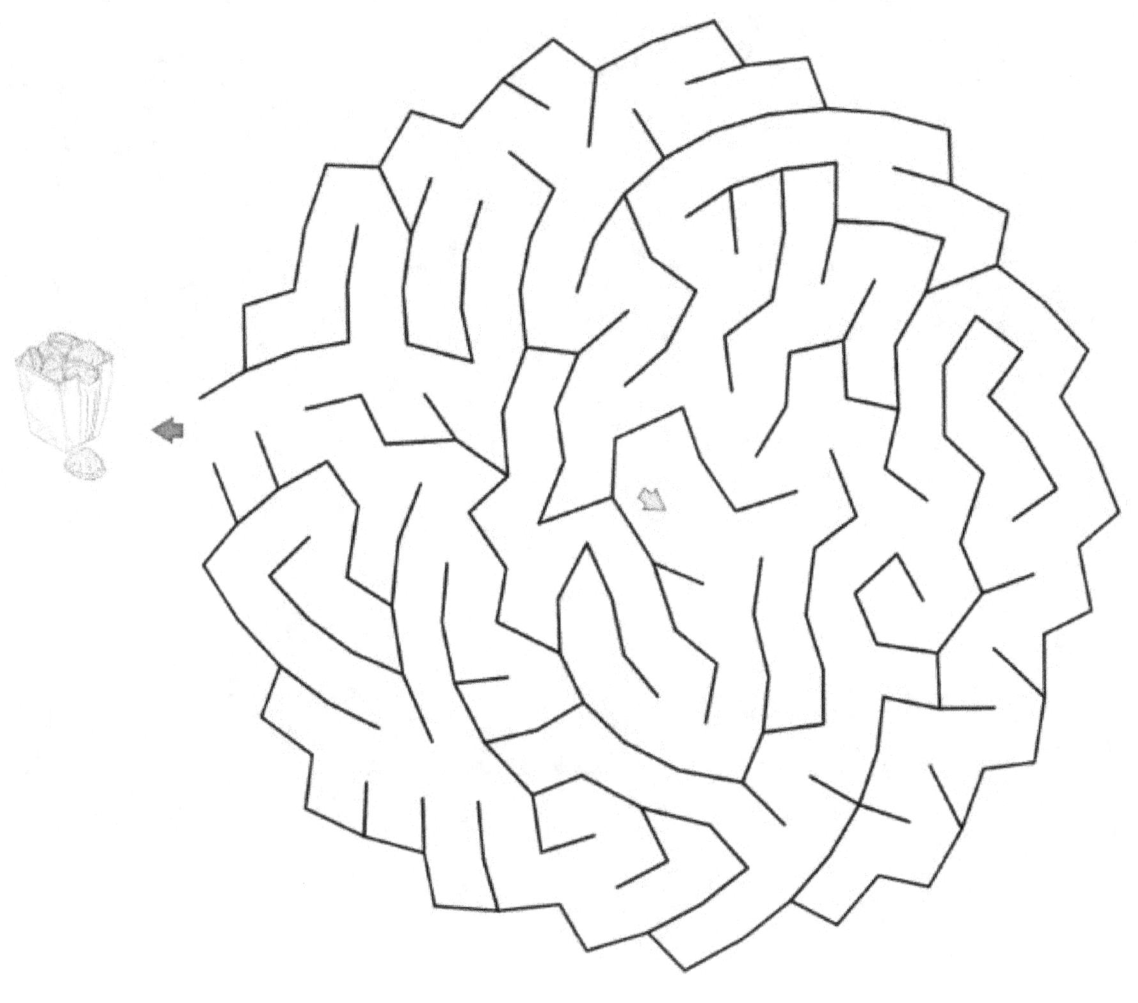

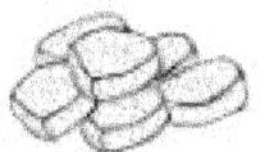